Dear Parent:
Your child's love of reading

Every child learns to read in a different way and at his or her own speed. You can help your young reader improve and become more confident by encouraging his or her own interests and abilities. You can also guide your child's spiritual development by reading stories with biblical values and Bible stories, like I Can Read! books published by Zonderkidz. From books your child reads with you to the first books he or she reads alone, there are I Can Read! books for every stage of reading:

SHARED READING
Basic language, word repetition, and whimsical illustrations, ideal for sharing with your emergent reader.

BEGINNING READING
Short sentences, familiar words, and simple concepts for children eager to read on their own.

READING WITH HELP
Engaging stories, longer sentences, and language play for developing readers.

READING ALONE
Complex plots, challenging vocabulary, and high-interest topics for the independent reader.

ADVANCED READING
Short paragraphs, chapters, and exciting themes for the perfect bridge to chapter books.

I Can Read! books have introduced children to the joy of reading since 1957. Featuring award-winning authors and illustrators and a fabulous cast of beloved characters, I Can Read! books set the standard for beginning readers.

A lifetime of discovery begins with the magical words **"I Can Read!"**

Visit www.icanread.com for information on enriching your child's reading experience.
Visit www.zonderkidz.com for more Zonderkidz I Can Read! titles.

"God said, 'Let the land produce all kinds of living creatures ... Let there be all kinds of them.' And that's exactly what happened."

—*Genesis 1:24–25*

ZONDERKIDZ

Rainforest Friends
Copyright © 2011 by Zonderkidz

Requests for information should be addressed to:
Zonderkidz, *Grand Rapids, Michigan 49530*

Library of Congress Cataloging-in-Publication Data

Rainforest friends.
    p. cm. — (LCR standards. Level 2)
    ISBN 978-0-310-72182-6 (softcover)
    1. Rain forest animals—Religious aspects—Christianity—Juvenile literature.
    BT746.R35 2011
    231.7—dc22   201001647

Editor: *Mary Hassinger*
Art direction & design: *Jody Langley*

13 14 15 /DSC/ 10 9 8 7 6 5 4 3

ZONDERkidz I Can Read! 2 READING WITH HELP

··· MADE·BY·GOD ···

Rainforest Friends

CONTENTS

God put more than

one-half of the earth's animals

in the rainforest.

He put colorful, graceful

parrots and creepy,

sneaky snakes like the …

ANACONDA!

The anaconda is the

largest snake in the world.

The longest known anaconda

was 37.5 feet long!

An anaconda can weigh 550 pounds

and be as big around

as a grown man.

Most anacondas are found

in swampy, tropical areas in

South America.

They like to be in water.

They live alone and can

live for ten or more years.

God put anacondas on earth

for a good reason.

They hunt and eat many

animals that could become

pests, like rodents and deer.

Anacondas hunt at night.

When they catch their food they

squeeze it until it stops

breathing.

Then the snake swallows it whole.

If the dinner is big, the anaconda

doesn't need to eat again

for a long time.

God made anacondas big

and strong.

He made another animal from

the rainforest big and strong.

He made the …

BENGAL TIGER!

Bengal tigers can be found

in the tropical forests of India.

They are big cats that like to swim!

The Bengal tiger runs

very fast too.

The Bengal tiger can grow very big.
They can be four-and-a-half to ten
feet long and weigh 500 pounds.

These big tigers have to eat a lot.

They catch animals like buffalo

and wild pigs using their good

nighttime vision, huge teeth,

and claws.

One tiger can eat up to 60 pounds

of meat at one time!

Bengal tigers like to be alone.
They sleep for up to eighteen
hours a day!
But some live in small groups
called streaks.

The Bengal tiger's roar is loud.

It can be heard up to

two miles away!

If people do not start
taking care of God's world,
the Bengal tigers might
not survive.
Another rainforest creature
that people must care for is
the special …

SPIDER MONKEY!

There are fourteen kinds
of spider monkeys.
These monkeys live in the
upper layer of the rainforests
in Central and South America.

Some of these spider monkeys

are called:

Red-faced spider monkey

White-front spider monkey

Mexican spider monkey

Spider monkeys live in
groups called troops.
They love to eat fruit.
They also like leaves,
flowers, and bugs.

The spider monkey's brain is
bigger than most monkeys'.
This large brain helps
them remember where to find
good food in the rainforest.

Spider monkeys can live

for 20 or more years.

They do not get too big—

they might be 14–26 inches long

and weigh 21–24 pounds.

Spider monkeys have four fingers

and no thumbs!

God gave spider monkeys long
tails to help them hold branches
as they swing around trees.
God makes sure that all of his
creatures have what they need
to live, just like the …

TOUCAN!

The toucan has a huge bill!
It can be very colorful and
can grow to be 1/3 of the
toucan's length.

The toucan uses its long bill
to get fruit, bird eggs, bugs, and
other food.
They eat fruit whole and spit
the seeds out—that helps more
trees grow!

Toucans live in the rainforests of South America. They build their nests in hollow tree parts.

Toucan babies are born
with no feathers at all.
The mother and dad birds
both take care of the babies.
The babies might have three
or four brothers or sisters!

Toucans like to live

together in groups

called flocks.

God made each rainforest
creature special.
He knows what they need
to live and grow.
He loves each one of these
special animals so much!